Fake Book Fundamentals

Exercises & Song Examples

Second Edition

by

Holly J. McCann

This book is dedicated to **all** of my students, former and present, younger and older, who helped me write this book by being my "test subjects"! Thank you!

Cover created by Lindsay J. Vaerenhall

Table of Contents:

Section Three - Intermediate to Advanced:

I. Playing a Fake Book Song on an Advanced Level

II. How to Build Your Own Arrangement of a Fake Book Song

III. Adding More Details to Your Arrangements

IV. Reference Section

Notes and Rests/Time Signatures/Lines and Spaces/Half Steps
and Whole Steps/Dictionary of Terms/**Chord Speller**

Forward

Many pianists struggle with reading notes on the staff, and I often hear from students who say they have difficulty reading the bass clef staff, and from people who have learned another instrument and have only learned the treble clef notes and not the bass clef notes.

I've been teaching private piano lessons for over 30 years, and several years ago I discovered a series of fake books that are all in the Key of C! With easy to read notes and chords, I discovered a perfect starting point for my students to make up their own arrangements! Once I started using these books with my students, grade 3-adult, I saw how easy it was for my students to read a melody in the right hand and learn how to play chords in the left hand. The C scale set of chords provides a "home base" to learn from. Once they advanced to a higher level, I made up exercises for them to learn how to put the chords in the right hand instead.

As the student is progressing through this book, I highly encourage the use of their own fake book for additional practice. There are easy fake books available, as well as more advanced fake books.

Below is a synopsis of how each section works in this book. This book is not just for beginning pianists, but for anyone who would like to learn to play from a lead sheet. This technique and knowledge opens up a WORLD of songs to you, the pianist.

Section One is for pianists who are starting out in a fake book for the first time. It is meant to be used in your piano lessons with your teacher, OR on your own. You may be a student in the second or third grade, a beginning student in high school, or an adult beginner. You may be an adult who has decided to go back to playing the piano after years of not playing. In this section you will learn all the basic major and minor chords, and how to play the melody in the right hand and the chords in the left hand.

Section Two is for pianists who have taken lessons with their teacher for a few years, generally from grade 4 through 6, or for teens and adults with some piano training. This section shows you how to turn the major and minor chords into inversion chords and how to fill in measures with blocked and broken chords in the left hand.

Section Three is for pianists who have been playing for many years and are generally in grades 7-12, or more advanced adults. This section will show you how to put the chords in the right hand by learning about melody and harmony, and fill in with more advanced left hand patterns.

The **Reference Section** has some valuable information about notes, time signatures, terms, and even includes a **CHORD SPELLER** in case you are trying to figure out chord names.

Section One

#1 The C Scale and Playing a Melody

All of the song examples in this book are based on the
C major scale, for ease in learning notes and chords.

There are many melodies that you will play with your right
hand in which you will have to **cross your thumb under**,
or **cross other fingers over**, in order to play the notes of
the melody smoothly. Learning the C scale will teach you
how to cross over and under within a melody.

The C scale is **all white keys** on the piano, starting with C
and ending with C. The fingering for the eight notes of the
scale are broken up into a **group of three and a group of
five**, so the pianist can play all eight notes with one hand.
The thumbs are finger number one.

Practice the C scale below, with your right hand, until you
are comfortable crossing under and crossing over in the
correct places.

The **seven basic chords of the C scale** are shown on the
following page and the letter names of the chords are the
basis for playing in different keys, such as D major, or A minor.

#2 Chords of the C Scale - Blocked

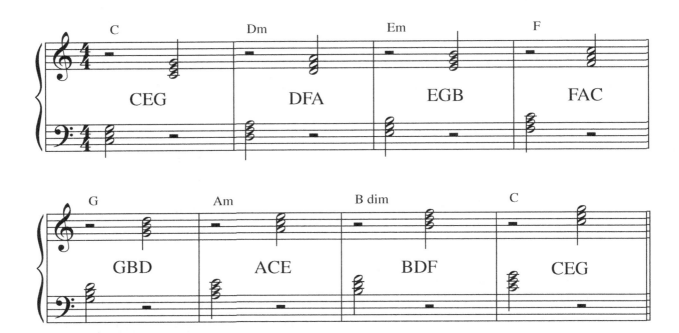

Each note of a scale is called a "degree". If you add two skipping letter names above each degree of the C scale (such as, CEG, DFA, etc.), you will form the chords of the C scale. These chords are called "**root position triad chords**", meaning that in a three note chord, the root (name of the chord) is on the bottom and the chord is written on **all lines or all spaces**.

In a fake book, the letters above the melody are called **"chord symbols"**. These chord symbols tell you which three letter names to play and which type of chord it is, major, minor, augmented, or diminished.

Memorize the letters of the chords so you can learn which chords share the same letter names, such as CEG and ACE, and because the chord letter names will **always stay the same**, some will just become **sharp or flat** depending upon the chord symbol.

Fingering: All triads are played with finger numbers 1, 3, and 5 in both hands.

Memorize: Some chords will sound Major (happy) and some will sound Minor (sad), but all chords of the C scale will be **white keys**.

Chords of the C Scale - Broken

Playing the same chords that you did on page 8, break up the chords into **separate notes** so they sound "broken".

In music, these broken chords are called **"arpeggios"** (the Italian word for harp).

#3 Major White Key Chords - Blocked

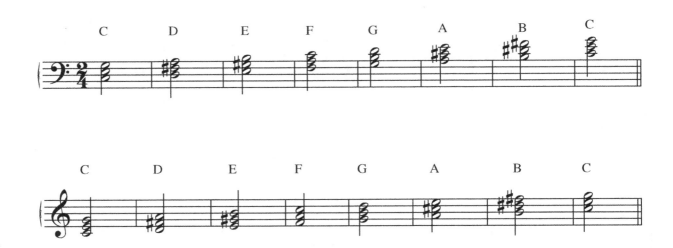

Major chords are generally used in songs and pieces of music that have a **happy** and cheerful sound.

Play the same chords as you did in Exercise #2, except in some chords you will have to **change one or two** of the keys to a black key to make the chord **sound "major"**.

Memorize: The C, F, and G chords are always **all white keys,** and the D, E, and A chords always have a **black key in the middle**.

The **exception** will be the **B chords**. The B major chord has **two black keys on the top**.

Major White Key Chords - Broken

Using the same chords that you did on page 10,
play all the chords like "arpeggios" or broken.

#4 Minor White Key Chords
Blocked and Broken

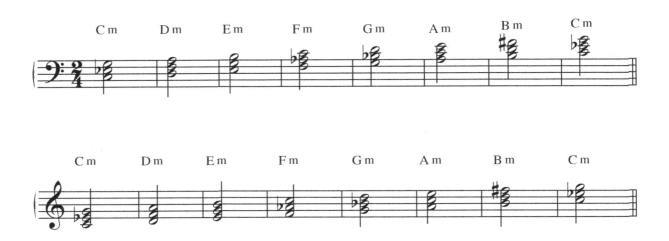

Minor chords are usually used in **sad** or scary pieces of music.

The middle note of the minor chord will be the **opposite color** of the major chord, and will be lowered one half step, which will make it **sound "minor"**.

After you practice the blocked minor chords, practice playing them in **broken** (arpeggio) form as you did in Exercise #3, page 11.

<u>Memorize</u>: The C, F, and G chords will now have a **black key in the middle** and the D, E, and A chords will be **all white keys**.

The B chord is the exception with **one black key on the top**.

#5 Primary Chords in the Key of C

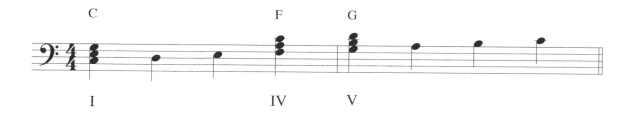

This example shows how triads (three notes played together) are built on the **first, fourth, and fifth** degrees of the C scale. The chords built on these three scale degrees are the **"primary"** chords of the C scale (C, F, and G chords), and will be the most **common chords** you use in the upcoming songs. They are considered primary because they are the only major chords in a major scale.

These primary chords are named tonic (I), sub-dominant (IV), and dominant (V). **Roman numerals** are used to indicate these chords.

To practice these three chords, put your **pinky on the bottom** of each of the three notes, C, F, or G, and practice playing all three notes together using the skipping finger pattern, 5-3-1, in the left hand.

Memorize: the three primary chords of the C scale, C, F, and G, will be the ONLY triads that are **all white keys**.

#6 The Easy Dominant 7th Chord

The Dominant 7th chord is a very important chord in all songs and pieces of music because it is the chord that **leads back to the "tonic" chord** (the chord built on the first degree of a scale).

The letter name of the **"dominant" chord** (the chord built on the fifth degree of a scale) is always **five steps above** the letter name of the tonic chord, for instance, C tonic and G dominant, D tonic A dominant, etc. When the tonic and dominant chords from each scale are played next to each other, they form a strong **"cadence"** (chords that sound like a musical phrase has ended).

Example #1 shows the G root position triad (V in the Key of C), and how to turn this triad into a full four note G7 chord (V7) by adding an additional line at the top of the chord. This chord now consists of a root, 3rd, 5th, and 7th.

Example #2 shows the two most important notes of that four note chord, the bottom note (the root) and the top note (the 7th). If those two notes are played **right next to each other**, with G on top and F on the bottom, they will form the **Easy G7 chord**.

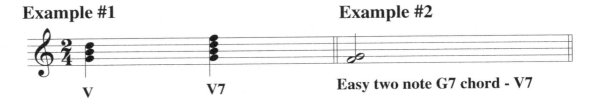

The exercise below shows each major white key chord and the easy dominant 7th chord that goes with it. These are combinations of **I and V7 chords** from each of these scales.

You may also practice this exercise using **minor** root position triads.

Memorize: To play **any easy 7th chord**, put your left hand thumb on the note that names the chord and play another note **one whole step down**.

#7 How to Play a Melody With Chords

Unless otherwise indicated in the music, a melody should always be played smooth and connected.

The exercise below will help you play a melody smoothly with the right hand, while you lift your left hand. Go slowly and make sure you **hear the melody notes holding** while you lift the left hand to change the chord.

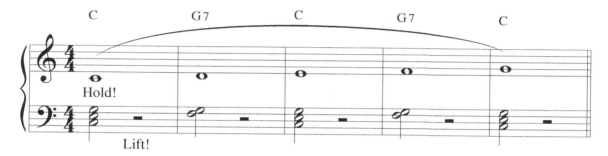

Song Example: Hot Cross Buns

This song example uses the combination of the tonic (I) and dominant (V) chords, C and G7 in the Key of C, and demonstrates how to play a melody in the right hand smoothly while lifting the left hand to change chords. The **quarter rests** indicate where to lift the left hand. Pretend that there are **slur lines** (see below) over the melody and play your right hand smoothly.

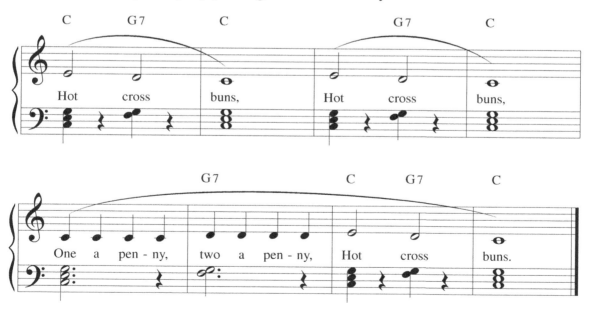

If you know how to play scales other than the C scale, try playing "Hot Cross Buns" in some **different keys** using the combination of tonic (I) and dominant 7th (V7) chords on page 14.

#8 Your First Fake Book Songs

It's time for you to start playing fake book melodies with blocked chords! In the next several song examples, you will be playing the melodies with the right hand and the root position triads with the left hand.

Think of the C chord as your **"home base" chord** and play the two note easy dominant 7th chord when you see the chord symbol "G7".

Memorize: When you see the **chord symbol above the melody**, play that two or three note chord with your left hand. The chord symbol above the melody may apply to several measures and will NOT be written in again until the chord changes so feel free to **add extra chords** on the first beat of a measure. You may play the melody **up one octave** if the notes go too far below middle C.

Practice the next three easy songs which use the C and G7 chords, and remember to play your right hand smoothly!

Lightly Row

Au Clair de la Lune

Moderately

French Folk Song

Sonata Theme

Andante

W.A. Mozart

#9 Song Example: Ode to Joy

In this famous tune, from Beethoven's 9th Symphony, you may want to try **two different versions** of the C chord. Since the first note of the melody starts on the middle note of the C chord, a two note C chord, C and G, sounds good with the E in the right hand melody.

In measure 3, you may want to try playing E and G, since C is in the right hand melody. This can be indicated by the chord symbol, C/E, meaning that **"E" will be the bottom note**.

Example #1

In Example #2, rests are shown in the left hand part to remind you to **lift your left hand between chords** so you have time to play the next one, and the right hand can play smoothly.

In measure 12, your left hand can play the melody note "G", even though it's written in the right hand part. Try the lead sheet on the next page, with your choice of left hand C chords!

Example #2

Ode to Joy

Joyfully

Ludwig van Beethoven

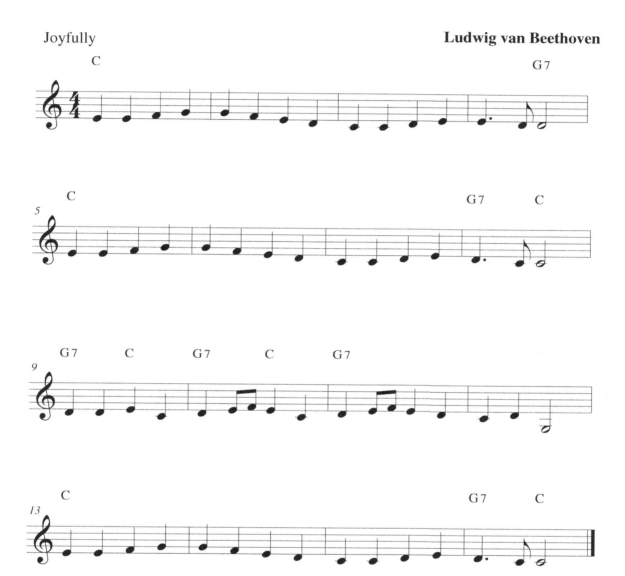

#10 Song Example:
When the Saints Go Marching In

In this song you will add the **F chord (IV)**, the chord built on the 4th note of the C scale, to the C chord and the two note G7 chord you have already learned. When you see the F chord symbol, simply **jump your left hand** up to the F chord (pinky on F).

<u>Note</u> that the first three notes of this song are NOT a full measure of four beats! This incomplete measure is called an *"upbeat"*, and many songs start with upbeats. This song starts on **beat number two**.

Practice this example, then try the whole song on the next page!

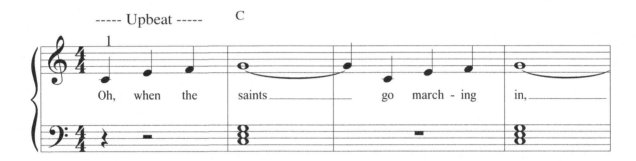

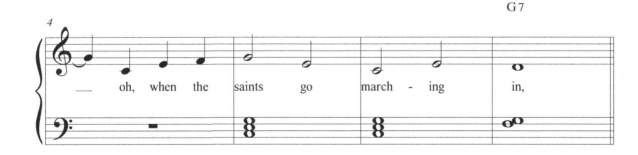

<u>Memorize</u>: The chord symbol above the melody may apply to several measures and will not be written again until the chord changes, so you may **add extra chords** as shown in the example above.

When the Saints Go Marching In

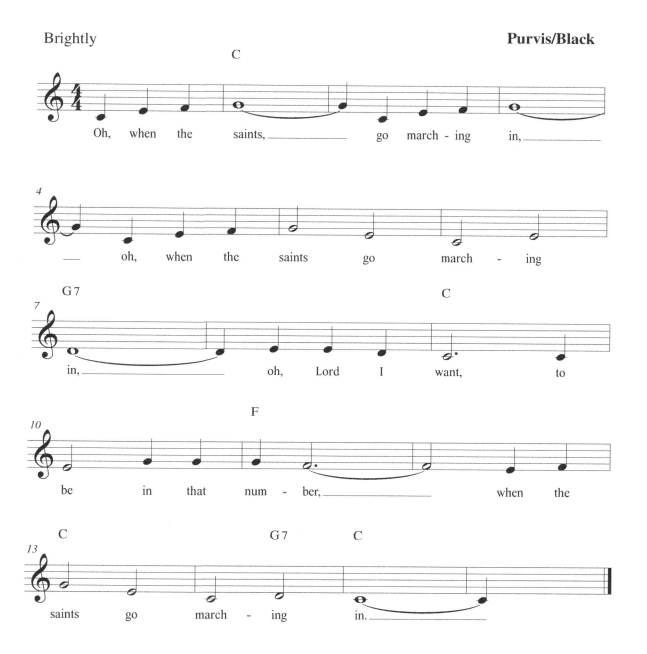

#11 Song Example: Jingle Bells

In this song example of "Jingle Bells", the three note C chord is shortened to a **two note chord** because the E of the C chord is in the right hand. The three notes, C, E, and G, are represented in both hands. Like you learned in Song Example #9, this is just another, and easier, way to play the C chord.

Make sure you remember to give your **left hand a beat** to lift up and change the chord so your right hand can play smoothly.

Jingle Bells

J. Pierpont

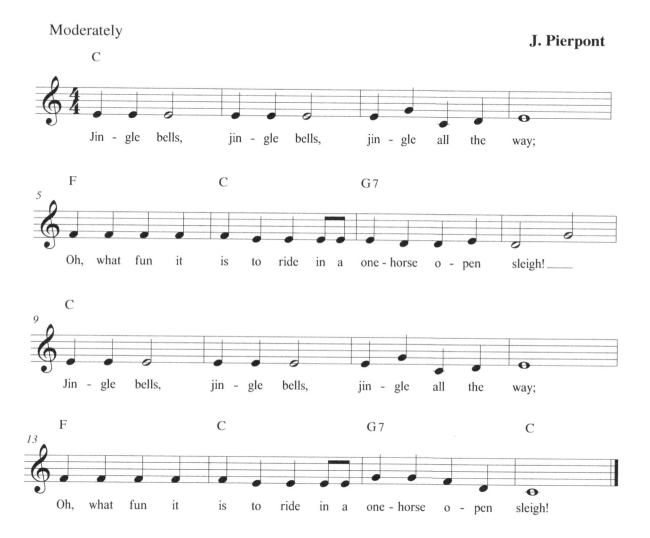

#12 Song Example: Yankee Doodle

This song example demonstrates how you can move your right hand **out of the five finger** position notes of CDEFG that you have been using for the past several songs.

In measure 4, keeping your thumb on middle C, you may **cross over** with finger #2 to play B.

In measure 7 and 8, cross over your thumb with finger #3 so you can play the **lower notes** below middle C.

Practice this example, following the finger numbers, then try the lead sheet on the next page.

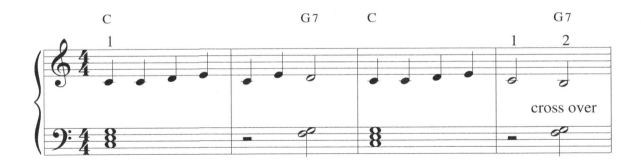

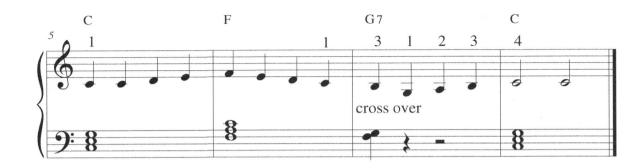

Note: you may play the melody up one octave if you don't like your hands to come too close to each other.

Yankee Doodle

#13 Song Example: Happy Birthday

This song is a perfect example of how to set your fingers up to play the **lowest note and the highest note** in the melody.

For each sentence, or phrase of music, your thumb (finger #1) can set on the lowest note while your pinky (finger #5) stays ready to play the highest note. Do this for every sentence and write the number in your music on the FIRST note of each sentence.

Practice the right hand of this melody to work out the fingering, and remember that you can extend your pinky and cross over your thumb to **reach more notes**!

Happy Birthday

Happily

Patty Hill and Mildred J. Hill

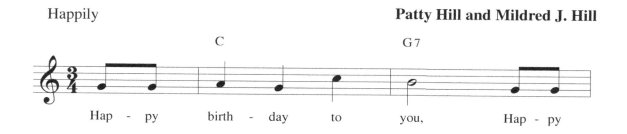

Hap - py   birth - day   to   you,   Hap - py

birth - day   to   you.   Hap - py   birth - day,   dear

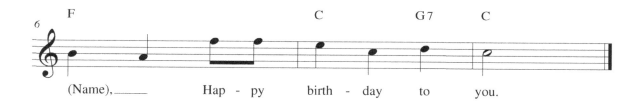

(Name),_____   Hap - py   birth - day   to   you.

#14 For He's A Jolly Good Fellow

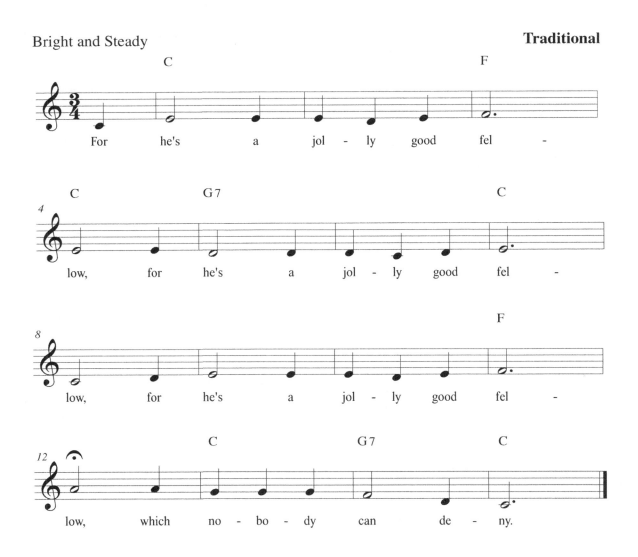

This is one final song to practice with left hand blocked chords.

If you feel you have mastered Section One, move on to Section Two to learn **left hand inversion chords** and more complicated right hand melodies.

Section Two

#1 Inversion Chords

A **root position triad** is a three note chord that is made up of **all lines or all spaces** on the staff, and the **bottom** note (root) names the chord.

An **inversion chord** is the **same three letter names** with the root (name of the chord) in a **different place** than on the bottom.

In the example below, two chords, F and G, are shown with their inversions. For example, the F chord (FAC), can be played as ACF or CFA. The <u>root F</u> has moved to the **top or the middle of the chord.**

These inversion chords are used so that you don't have to move your left hand away from the C chord, which is your "home base" chord. It is easier to play chords as **close to the C chord** as possible.

FAC   ACF   CFA   GBD   BDG   DGB

#2 Inversion Chords in the Key of C

Example #1

C remains the same on the bottom! *G stays the same on the top!* *Thumb moves up one step!* *The 7th (F) is added to the G chord!*

Example #2

In this exercise, you can practice playing the **most common** inversion chords that are near the "home base" C chord. Notice that the easy two note G7 chord now has an extra note (the 3rd of the chord) on the bottom to make it sound fuller.

Repeat the measures in Example #1 until you are very comfortable switching chords.

Example #2 combines these chords together into a <u>chord progression</u>. Inversion chords are used to keep the F, Am, and G7 chords close to the "home base" C chord.

<u>Memorize</u>: The C, Am, and F chords all share a common letter name, the C on the bottom.

<u>Fingering</u>: If the inversion chord has a **skip** (skipping a key) on the top, don't forget to use finger #2 in the middle!

#3 Song Example: Country Gardens

Example #1

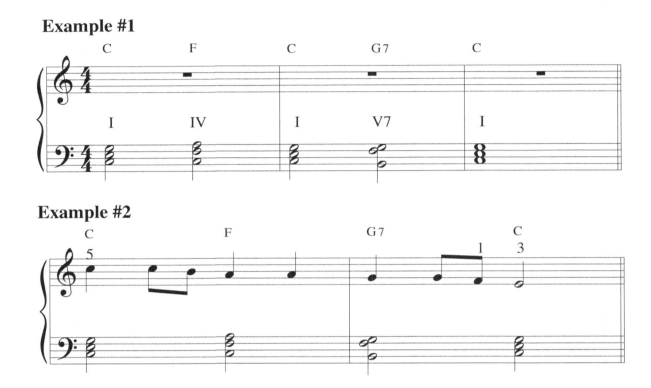

Example #2

Example #1 above shows a common chord progression using the three most important chords of the C scale, C, F, and G7. These chords, known as **primary chords**, are built on the 1st (tonic I), 4th (sub-dominant IV), and 5th (dominant V) degrees of any scale. These primary chords are also given **roman numerals** as shown in the first example.

Example #2 above shows you how to apply the C chord progression, using the three primary chords, to "Country Gardens".

Practice both lines until comfortable and then try the whole piece on the next page.

Country Gardens

Moderately

Old English Dance

#4 Song Example:
Twinkle, Twinkle, Little Star

Here is a very familiar tune in which you can practice the Key of C chord progression with the **three primary chords**, C, F, and G7.

If you are learning other scales besides the C scale, this is a perfect song to learn how to play in a **different key** with a different set of primary chords. This is called *"transposing"*!

Practice this song example and try the lead sheet on the next page.

Twinkle, Twinkle, Little Star

Gently   **J. Taylor**

#5 Song Example:
My Country, 'Tis of Thee

Here is another song to practice playing the three primary chords, C, F, and G7, of the C scale.

Make sure that you work out the fingering of the melody on your lead sheet!

My Country, 'Tis of Thee

#6 Song Example: Morning

On page 31, you learned the A minor chord inversion with the C on the bottom, because it is the closest A minor chord to the C chord. In measure 15 in the example above, if you use the E root position triad with E on the bottom, you can use the A minor inversion chord with the **E on the bottom**. After the A minor chord, a root position G chord sounds like a strong ending to that phrase!

Memorize: The root or inversion chords you use in your left hand will be determined by the **chords that come before or after**, and, always look for common letter names.

Morning

Peacefully

Edvard Grieg

#7 Broken or Blocked Fill-In Chords

The following three parts will show you **left hand patterns** that you can use to fill in a measure with broken or blocked chords if the right hand is playing a **long melody note**.

Get creative and add as many chords as you like to your songs.

This is how you can start making up your own arrangements!

Part I: uses broken chords. Practice song examples "Down in the Valley" and "Shepherd's Hymn".

Part II: uses a dotted rhythm blocked chord pattern. Practice song example "Michael, Row the Boat Ashore".

Part III: uses a broken chord accompaniment. Practice song examples "Take Me Out to the Ball Game" and "Can-Can".

Once you master these song examples, continue to the next several song examples and use any of the left hand styles listed above. You can also go back to the lead sheets in Section One and the beginning of Section Two to practice adding more blocked and broken chords to your arrangements!

Part I: Broken Fill-In Chords

The example below demonstrates how to play a broken chord as fill-in on the long right hand notes.

Repeat each measure of the example below until you are comfortable playing these patterns. These patterns are for songs that are slower or pretty and more flowing.

Song Example: Down in the Valley

Try the song example for "Down in the Valley" above, practice the lead sheet on the next page, and apply the **same patterns** of broken chords to "Shepherd's Hymn".

Down in the Valley

Traditional

Slow, waltz tempo

Shepherd's Hymn
(from the 6th Symphony)

Moderately

Ludwig van Beethoven

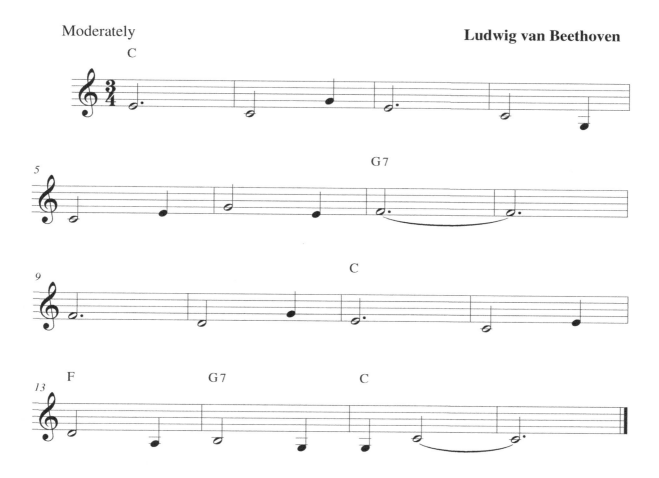

Part II: Blocked Fill-In Chords

The example below is for songs that would use a more rhythmic pattern because of the style of the song, for instance a **rock and roll, pop, or contemporary song**.

Repeat this line until you memorize how the rhythm sounds and then try the song example of "Michael, Row the Boat Ashore" below.

Song Example:
"Michael, Row the Boat Ashore"

Michael, Row the Boat Ashore

Moderately

Traditional Folk Song

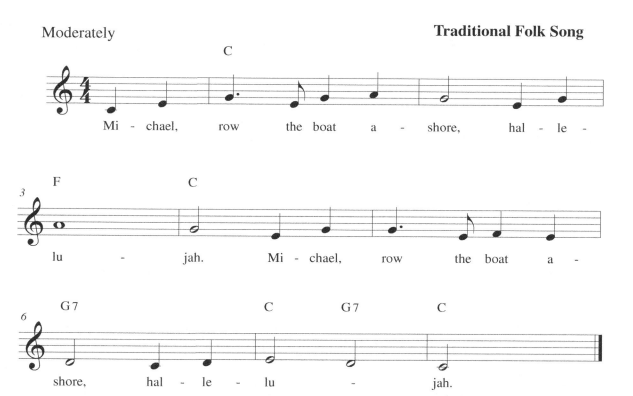

Part III: Broken Chord Accompaniment

Example #1

Example #2

The left hand chord accompaniment patterns above, are a good example of how to fill-in with chords on longer right hand notes.

Example #1 shows you how to play three common left hand patterns, in different time signatures, using **root position triads**.

Example #2 shows you how to play the C chord progression, I IV V7 I, with **inversion chords** in this style.

These left hand patterns are commonly called the **"oom pah"** patterns. For instance, if there are 4 beats in a measure, the pattern would be "oom pah pah pah".

Practice these patterns and then try out the song examples of "Take Me Out to the Ball Game" and "Can-Can" on the next page. The full lead sheets for **both songs** follow the song examples.

Song Examples:

Take Me Out to the Ball Game

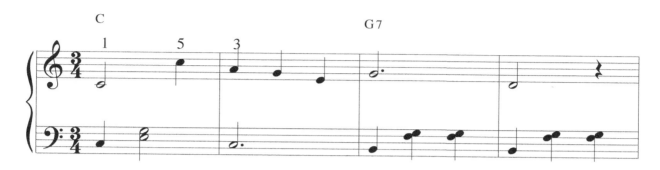

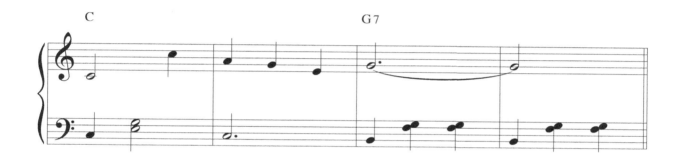

Can-Can

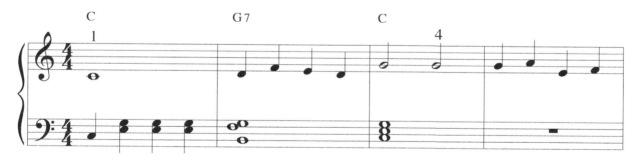

Take Me Out to the Ball Game

Can-Can

Quickly

Jacques Offenbach

#8 Song Example: Prelude, op. 28, no. 7

The song example below is **one possible** arrangement you can play of this pretty melody written by Frederic Chopin, a Romantic era composer. The broken chord accompaniment from page 46, works well with this piece.

Make sure you figure out the fingering for each phrase according to the **lowest note and highest note** of each phrase. It may be awkward to put your thumb on a black key melody note, so try using a longer finger such as finger #2, then cross your thumb under to get to the higher notes.

Prelude, op. 28, no. 7

Andantino

Frederic Chopin

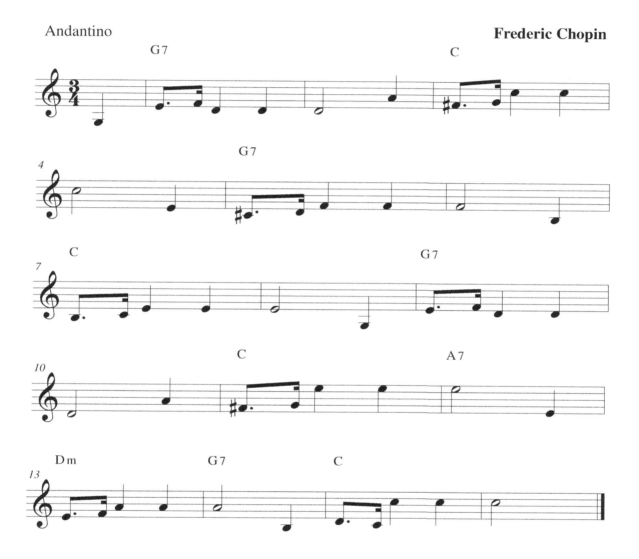

#9 Song Example: Sleeping Beauty Waltz

Here are two examples of how to add fill-in chords to the longer melody notes.

Example #1 uses the broken chord accompaniment from page 46.
Example #2 uses broken chords from page 41.

Example #1

Example #2

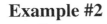

Sleeping Beauty Waltz

Andante

Peter Illyich Tchaikovsky

#10 Song Example: Minuet (from Don Giovanni)

This piece of music by Mozart, from his famous opera "Don Giovanni", starts out with the "home base" C chord, but moves to a new "home base" chord in measure 6, because the D7 chord in measure 5 is the **dominant (V) chord in the key of G.** The G chord now becomes the "home base" chord and can be played using a root position triad. In measures 5-8, you can play the chord progression using the three primary chords in the key of G (G, C and D7).

This use of triads **outside of the key of the piece,** happens quite often in music.

Fingering: try NOT to put your thumb on a black key in the melody unless necessary!

Memorize: If the chord symbols indicate a change in the "home base" chord, make sure that you go back to the "home base" C chord when you see the **G7 chord symbol**!

Minuet (from Don Giovanni)

Stately

W.A. Mozart

#11 Song Example: The Entertainer

This famous tune by the "King of Ragtime", Scott Joplin, is in **"cut time"**, meaning that the notes look like they are written in 4/4 time but the feel of the piece is in 2/2, two beats per measure instead of four. Note the **abbreviation** symbol for 2/2 at the beginning of this piece.

In Example #1, measures 1-3, the C chord in measure 1 becomes a **C dominant 7th chord (V7)**, which leads to the F chord. A C chord could be used in measure 2, but the C7 chord is a stronger "pull" to the F chord, because it's a dominant 7th chord. This happens quite often in music.

Instead of playing the note G with your thumb in the C chord, **play a Bb to make it dominant** and that will lead directly to the F inversion chord in measure 3.

Example #1

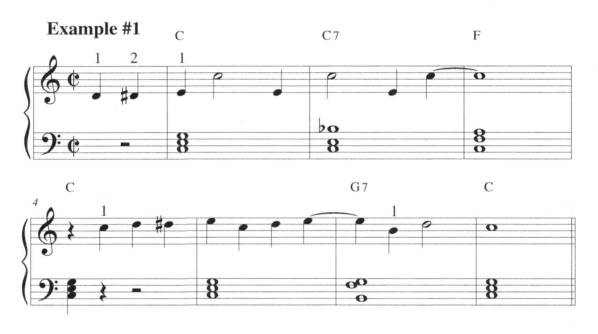

Example #2

The Entertainer

Not too fast

Scott Joplin

#12 Ending a Song or Piece of Music

Example #1: Hand over Hand Arpeggios

Example #2: Hand Replace Hand Arpeggios

Example #3: C to Csus to C

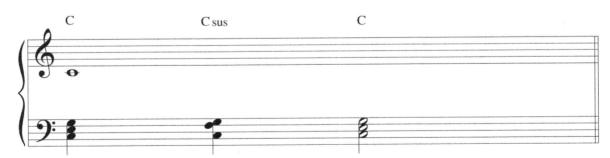

The "sus" chord (suspension) is used by composers to set-up **tension to the tonic** chord. Replace the E in the C chord with F, then resolve the chord back to CEG.

Section Three

Playing a Fake Book Song on an Advanced Level

The more advanced way to play a fake book song is to shift the chords from the **left hand to the right hand.** Harmony notes are added to the melody notes to create **two or three note chords** in the right hand.

Example #1 and 2 on the following page, show the difference between playing chords in the left hand and playing chords in the right hand.

The next several exercises in this section will show you how to play chords in the right hand and **single note patterns in the left hand** to accompany the right hand. Once you are comfortable with these exercises, you will be ready to make your own advanced arrangement of a lead sheet.

The first five measures of "Arioso" by J. S. Bach are shown below with left hand chords that follow the chord symbols.

Example #1

Below are the same five measures of "Arioso" with harmony notes added **below the melody notes** to form chords in the right hand and single notes in the left hand instead of chords.

Example #2

Every lead sheet can be played with chords in the left hand OR the right hand, usually **not in both hands** at the same time. The pianist may decide which style to use according to the piece of music and their pianistic ability.

#1 Adding Harmony to a Melody Note

The more advanced way to play a melody in a fake book is to add harmony notes **BELOW the melody notes** to form chords in the right hand instead of the left hand.

To review: a chord is made up of three notes, the **Root, the 3rd, and the 5th**. For instance, in a C chord, C is the root, E is the 3rd, and G is the 5th. Parts I, II, and III of this section will show you how to add harmony notes BELOW each one of the notes of a chord, the root, the 3rd, or the 5th.

An interval in music is the **space** between two notes. The intervals of 3rds and 6ths sound more pleasing to the ear, so these intervals are called harmony. These are the intervals you should play when forming a right hand chord (three notes and six notes below the melody).

Do not play any intervals of 4ths and 5ths, (**four or five notes** below the melody) because these intervals are not considered harmony and are NOT pleasing to the ear.

Part I

If the **melody note is a root note**, such as C of the C chord, the ONLY choice for a harmony note is **six notes below the root**.

Practice each line, adding the interval of a 6th below to make a **two note chord**.

Major

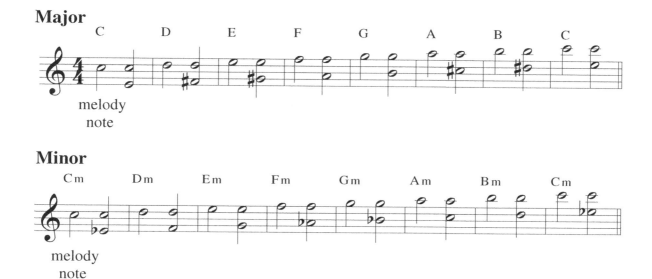

Minor

Memorize: If the chord symbol matches the melody note, for instance, C chord and a C melody note or a G chord and a G melody note, you can ONLY play the **6th below** for harmony.

For major chords, any chord that is NOT C, F, and G (which are always all white keys), will have a black key on the bottom.

If the chord symbol is minor, play the opposite of major, so now the C, F, and G chords will have the **black key on the bottom**.

Part II

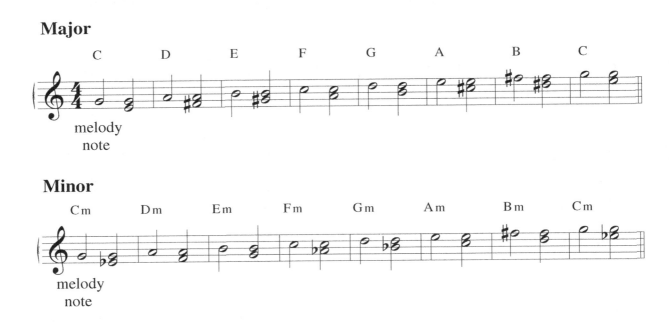

When the melody note is the **5th of the chord**, which in the C chord would be G, the ONLY possible harmony note you can play is a **skip below** (interval of a 3rd).

Memorize: If the **chord symbol is D, E, A, or B**, you must play a black key as the skip below the melody note! If the chord symbol is C, F, or G, **both notes are WHITE**. For minor chords, do the opposite.

Part III

Major

melody
note

Minor

melody
note

When the melody note is the 3rd of the chord, which in the
C chord would be E, you have **two possible** harmony notes,
a **skip (a 3rd) or a 6th below** the melody note.

Try playing the SKIP first, since that's easier to remember.
If the chord before or after is a 6th, then you can try playing
the 6th below instead, so all the chords sound like they go
together.

Memorize: If you add the interval of a 3rd or 6th below
these melody notes (the 3rd of any chord), it will always
be a **WHITE** key, except for the **two B chords**.

#2 Left Hand Octave Pattern

This is the **"all-purpose"** left hand pattern to use when the right hand plays the melody with harmony notes added to it. This pattern uses the root and the 5th of the chord but not the 3rd. Since the 3rd note of any chord determines whether that chord is major or minor, the **all-purpose left hand pattern** can be used with ANY chord that the right hand plays.

These left hand patterns are **all white keys** and should be repeated until you are very comfortable playing them.

Memorize: The first and last note of the octave pattern are the same letter name one octave apart and the middle note is FIVE steps up from the bottom note.
Example: C G C, D A D, E B E, etc.

Fingering: Use **finger numbers 5-2-1** for each measure and play smooth and connected. Try the damper pedal to practice pedaling.

#3 Left Hand Octave Pattern
with White Key Chords

Practice playing the right hand chords of the C scale with the left hand octave pattern.

This exercise uses **all white keys** and is a good introduction to playing hands together using the left hand octave pattern.

Use the damper pedal to **practice pedaling** and to make the exercise sound smooth.

#4 Left Hand Octave Pattern
with Right Hand Major Chords

Practice playing the right hand **major chords** with the left hand octave pattern.

Memorize: The B chords are always different than the other chords. Since the B major or minor chord always has a **black key on the top** (the 5th of the chord), the B octave pattern must always have a **black key in the middle**.

#5   Left Hand Octave Pattern with Right Hand Minor Chords

Practice playing right hand **minor chords** with the left hand octave pattern.

Notice that the left hand **rhythmic pattern has changed**, so you can practice varying the pattern.

How to Build Your Own Arrangement of a Fake Book Song

Now that you have learned how to add harmony notes to melody notes and how to do the octave pattern in the left hand, you can put together your own advanced arrangement of any song!

The song example "Amazing Grace" will show you how to build an arrangement step by step. After practicing "Amazing Grace", **study the additional song examples** to gain more practice.

Once you have the basics down, move on and practice the exercises to learn the black key chords, diminished and augmented chords, 7th chords, and an expanded left hand octave pattern so you can add more details to your arrangements.

#6 Song Example: Amazing Grace

Part I - Adding Harmony Notes

Example #1

Example #2

Example #1 shows the melody of "Amazing Grace" as it would look in a fake book.

Example #2 shows you how to add the **harmony notes BELOW** the melody notes.

Memorize: Whenever you see a chord symbol, add a harmony note **below the melody note**. The easiest way is to **add a skip below** the melody note unless the melody note and the chord symbol match. In that case, you can only add a **6th below**, as in Part I of #1, p. 63.

Make sure that the harmony notes you add are **letters in the chord symbol** which means that sometimes a 3rd or a 6th below will NOT work.

If a measure does not have a chord symbol over it, it is the **same chord** as the measure before and you may add another harmony note to the melody note.

Part II - Adding the Left Hand
Octave Pattern

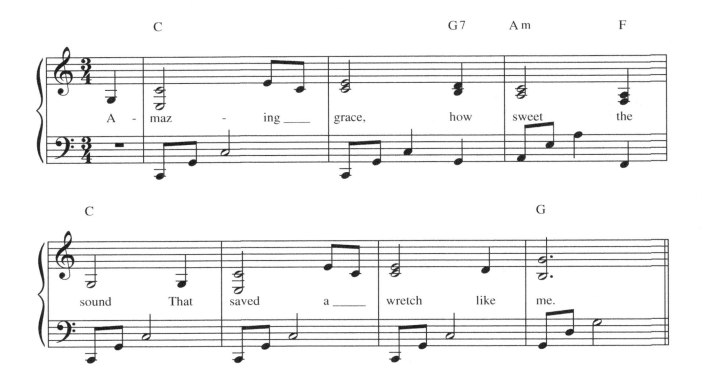

You can now add the left hand **octave pattern** to the melody/harmony chords that the right hand learned in Part I.

You can easily fit all **three notes** of the left hand octave pattern on the first two beat chord of each measure if you use the **8th note** pattern (see page 69).

Memorize: The octave pattern you play in the left hand should match the chord symbol, for instance, a chord symbol **G**, would be a **G octave pattern.**

Amazing Grace

Moderately slow

Traditional/Newton

#7 Song Example: Lullaby

Like you practiced in "Amazing Grace", this song example of "Lullaby" shows you how to fill in the left hand octave patterns on the longer, first beat right hand chords in some measures.

A simple **bass note in the left hand** can be played in measures with several melody notes.

A harmony note in the right hand is added **below the melody, using intervals of 3rds and 6ths** on the first beat of each measure.

Lullaby

Andante

Johannes Brahms

#8 Song Example: Ave Maria

SLASH CHORDS in music are usually used if the composer wants a "walking bass" sound in their music. Your left hand plays the **second letter** of the chord symbol **after** the slash, and your right hand plays the letter name of the chord **before** the slash.

If you are playing chords in the left hand instead, you may place the second letter of the slash chord as the bottom note of the chord. For instance, in the chord G/B, B will become the **bottom note of the chord**.

In this song example of "Ave Maria", the left hand fills in with quarter notes according to the **second letter of the chord symbol**. This way you can hear the bass notes walking down and up. You may also choose to play this song with octave patterns according to the **first letter** of the chord symbol.

Practice this song example and then try the whole song on the next page.

Ave Maria

Charles Gounod

#9 Song Example: Symphony No. 9
(The New World)

Example #1

Example #2

Example #1 above is one possible arrangement for "The New World Symphony Theme". You may use as many octave patterns as you want, to fill in on the longer right hand notes, or just use a repeated bass note like the example above.

Note that the C+ chord is an augmented chord, so the only note you need to change in the octave pattern is the **middle note**. For a C augmented chord the G becomes a G#, and for a C diminished chord, the G becomes a Gb (see Exercise #15).

Example #2 of this song example (measures 21-22 on the lead sheet) shows the use of **slash chords** (see Song Example #8). Instead of using octave patterns in the left hand, you may choose to play the **second letter of the chord symbol** as the bass note.

Symphony No. 9 (The New World)

Largo

Antonin Dvorak

#10 Song Examples: Who's Sorry Now? and Come Back to Sorrento

"Who's Sorry Now?", made famous by singer Connie Francis in 1957, shows how dotted rhythm can be played in the left hand as a more **rhythmic fill-in** for a pop song. This kind of bass line can be played for any contemporary, pop, or rock and roll song or piece of music.

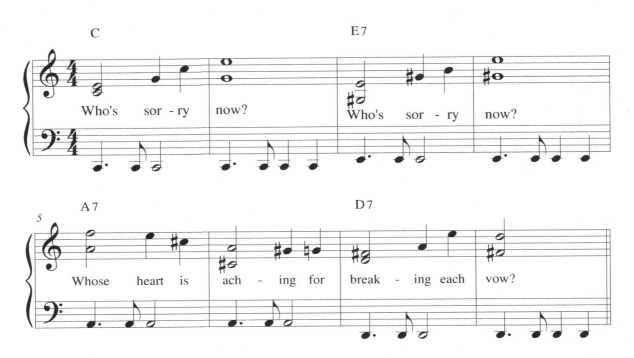

Once you are comfortable with the techniques you learned on pages 71-80, adding a harmony note to the right hand melody and the left hand accompaniment patterns, try "Come Back to Sorrento", a famous Neapolitan song from Italy, on page 82.

This song uses the **Cm-Fm-G7 chord progression** at the beginning.

Who's Sorry Now?

Snyder/Kalmar/Ruby

Come Back to Sorrento

Ernesto de Curtis

Expressively

Adding More Details To
Your Arrangements

The next several pages have exercises to help you add more details to your arrangements and to make your playing sound even **more advanced**.

The first exercise expands the white key octave pattern in the left hand, for a more advanced fill-in.

The next set of exercises are designed to teach you the black key chords, in addition to the white key chords you learned in Section One, and to play ALL the chords in root **and** inversion position, so you can play the right hand melody/harmony with FULL chords instead of just two notes.

Practice all of these exercises until you are **very comfortable** playing them and then you will be ready to move on and try the song examples.

#11 Expanded Left Hand Patterns

These exercises show more advanced examples of how to fill in with your left hand if your right hand is playing a **long melody note**. These examples can be played in two, three, or four beat patterns.

Part I is the octave pattern with step crossovers that sound major or minor. The **last three notes** of the pattern form the first three notes of a major or minor scale (do re mi). The top note of the minor pattern will be **lowered one half step** from the major.

Part II is like the octave pattern but instead of playing the top note as the octave up from the bottom note, play one skip higher, which is the third of the chord, and will **determine whether that pattern is major or minor**. That note is the interval of a 10th above the first note of the pattern.

Memorize: Step crossovers: for a major chord symbol, play the octave pattern and cross over two whole steps **(W+W)**. For minor, play the octave pattern and cross over one whole step plus one half step **(W+H)**.

If you are playing the octave pattern with a 10th, remember that some chord symbols will require a **black key** (refer to chords in Section One).

Part I - Step Crossovers

Major

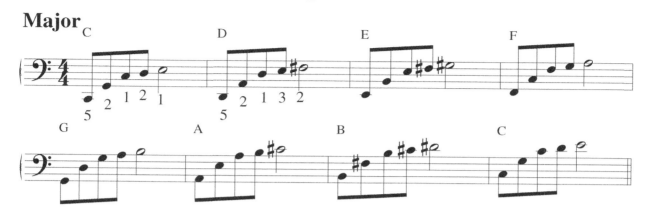

Minor

Part II - Adding the Tenth

Major

Minor

#12 Learning Chromatic Chords

Parts I, II, and III

Now that you know all of the major and minor white key chords and the basic left hand octave pattern, it's time to learn all of the other chords (black key chords).

The musical term **"chromatic"** means to go up or down by half steps (see Reference Section #4). The exercises in **Parts I, II, and III**, start on the C chord and move up by half steps to the next chord.

The chords between the white key chords (from this book's Section One) are called "black key chords" because their **root note is a black key**. Many of the chords will have two names, for instance, C# is the same as Db.

Exercises for the left hand chromatic octave patterns follow the right hand chord exercises.

Part I - Playing the Outside Notes

The easiest way to learn all the root chords (white and black), is to play **only the outside notes** first and leave out the middle notes. Using fingers #1 and #5 and starting on C, move up by half steps, practicing both hands.

Note that some of these chords may have **two names**, for instance, Db/C#, F#/Gb, Ab/G#, and the key of the song/piece will determine which chord symbol is used.

Memorize: ALL of the two note chords in this exercise are either a **white to a white** key or a **black to a black** key, EXCEPT for the **two B chords** which are opposite color, black/white, or white/black.

Part II - Adding the Inside Note

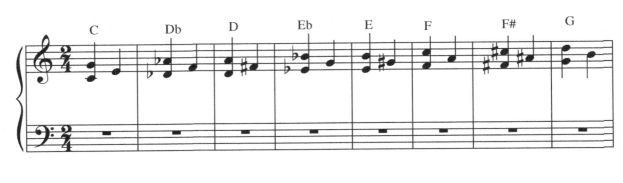

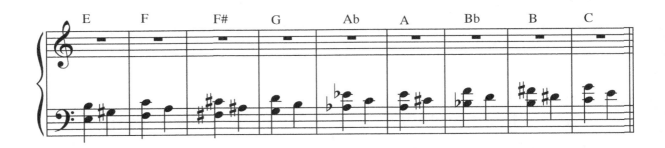

In this exercise, you will continue to play the same two note chords as in Part I, thinking white/white or black/black, except for the two B chords (which are ALWAYS the opposite color), and add in **the middle note separately**.

Fingering: **Feel the middle finger** (#3) moving up by half steps while fingers #1 and 5 play the outer two notes. These are all **major chords**. If the chord sounds minor, then the middle note you played is **wrong**.

Part III - The Whole Chord

After you have practiced repeatedly on Part I and Part II, you can now play **all three notes together** to form the <u>chromatic major chords</u>.

Watch the chord symbols above the chords as you play them so you can **learn and memorize the chord** you are playing.

To change these chords to minor, simply <u>lower</u> the middle note **one half step**.

Remember, the **bottom note** names the chord because the notes are **all line or all space notes**.

#13 Left Hand Chromatic Octave Pattern

Example #1

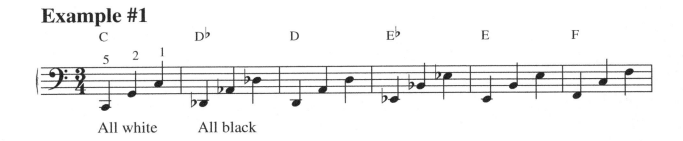

This exercise shows how the left hand can play the octave pattern **chromatically**, like the right hand chords in Exercise #12.

Practice Example #1 until you are comfortable playing the left hand chromatic octave pattern.

Examples #2 and 3 include the major and minor root position chords in the right hand. Note that the notes of the left hand octave pattern do not change, but the **rhythmic pattern varies**.

Memorize: **ALL three notes** of the chromatic octave pattern are either **all white or all black keys**, EXCEPT for the two **B patterns**, whose middle note will be the **opposite color** from the outside two notes.

Example #2 - Major

Example #3 - Minor

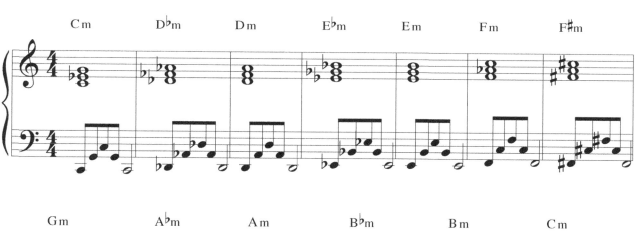

#14 Chromatic Inversion Chords

Part I - 1st Inversion - Major

The following exercises are the **inversion chords** of the right hand chromatic root position chords you learned in Exercise #12.

Notice that the left hand octave pattern changes for Part I, II, III, and IV, so you can practice varying the rhythmic patterns.

Memorize: When you play 1st inversion chords, the name of the chord is **on the top**. When you play 2nd inversion chords, the name of the chord is **in the middle**.

Part II - 2nd Inversion - Major

Part III - 1st Inversion - Minor

Part IV - 2nd Inversion - Minor

#15 Diminished and Augmented Chords

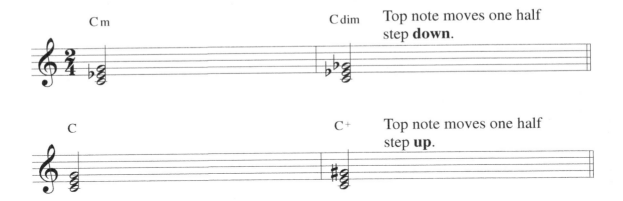

In a fake book, you will often see chords that are different than major and minor. Many of these different chords will be **diminished and augmented.**

To form a diminished triad, start with a minor root position chord and simply **lower** the top note (the fifth) one half step. The chord symbol will have a "dim" next to the letter (Cdim). If the note you are lowering is already flat, it would become **double flat.**

To form an augmented triad, start with a major root position chord and simply **raise** the top note (the fifth) one half step. The chord symbol will have a "+" or "aug" next to the letter (C+). If the note you are raising is already sharp, it would become **double sharp.**

Memorize: The "all-purpose" left hand octave patterns, that were all white or all black, except for the B patterns, will now have a **black or white** key in the pattern according the the chord symbol.

If you need help with the letter names of these chords, see **#6 Chord Speller** in the Reference Section.

Part 1: Diminished Chords

Part II: Augmented Chords

Putting It All Together

In the next few song examples you can put all that you have learned in this book, **together in one song/piece**.

You can practice using two or three note chords in the right hand melody, and octave patterns in the left hand with step crossovers to fill in.

Song Example #19 will show you how to play 7th chords and you can try an easy arrangement of a jazz-style song.

Three new endings will complete your arrangements.

Once you have mastered all of the components in this book, you can try any fake book song/piece you like!

#16 Song Example: Barcarolle

Example #1

Example #2

This famous duet from the opera "The Tales of Hoffmann",
is a good example of **6/8 rhythm**, and how to fill in the
longer right hand notes with the left hand octave pattern.

Example #1 is measures 1-4 on the lead sheet.
Example #2 is measures 17-20 on the lead sheet.

Memorize: 6/8 rhythm has a two beat feel and is **counted
in two**. Each octave pattern will feel like a "triplet" (three
notes that equal ONE beat).

Practice these examples and then try the entire piece on
the next page.

Barcarolle (from The Tales of Hoffmann)

Moderately

Jacques Offenbach

Barcarolle (from The Tales of Hoffmann)

#17 Song Example: Greensleeves

In this song example of "Greensleeves", measures 17-24, full three note chords are used in the right hand when there is a chord symbol change. You may also use full chords on any other melody notes.

Octave patterns with step crossovers in the left hand, work very well as fill-in on the longer notes of the melody.

By choosing how many notes to add in a right hand chord and the type of left hand pattern to use, you are forming **your own arrangement**.

Greensleeves

Flowing

English Folk Song

#18 Song Example: Fairest Lord Jesus

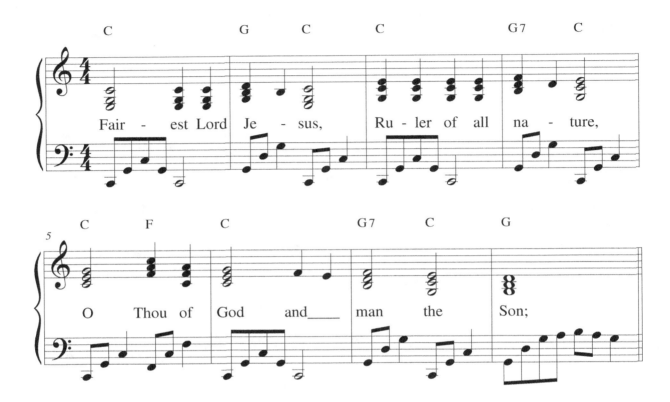

This famous church hymn has been given more of a piano-style arrangement rather than an organ-style arrangement with the use of the **8th note pattern** in the left hand for a more flowing sound.

Single bass notes can be used in the left hand for a more "blocked" organ-style sound.

Full **three note** chords in the right hand give this piece a very full, warm sound.

Fairest Lord Jesus

Tenderly

Music from Schlesische Volkslieder

#19 Seventh Chords and How to Play an Easy Jazz Arrangement

Example #1

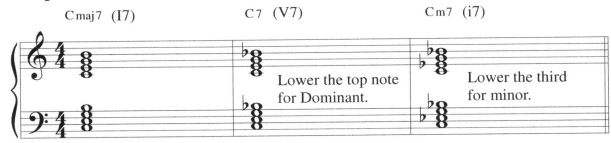

Example #2

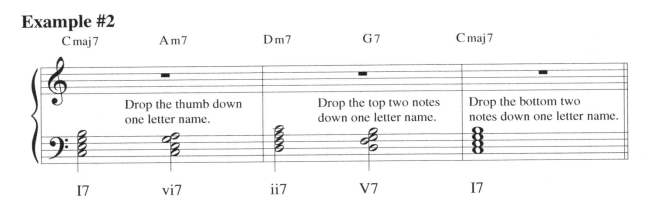

The three chords in Example #1 are the most common 7th chords that you will see in a fake book, **major, dominant, and minor**. These chords have an added interval of a 3rd on the top of the major or minor root position triads to turn them into **four note chords**. The chord is now made up of a **root, 3rd, 5th, and 7th**.

The tonic major 7th (I7) chord follows the key signature of the major scale.
The tonic minor 7th (i7) chord follows the key signature of the minor scale.
The dominant 7th (V7) chord follows the key signature of the <u>tonic</u> degree.

Example #2 shows you the most common chord progression in a jazz style song, using all three types of 7th chords, major, dominant, and minor, and is in the Key of C. This chord progression uses the **chords built on the 1st, 2nd, 5th, and 6th degrees** of any scale. Adding the 7th to the triads built upon these degrees, gives the piece a jazz sound.

<u>**Memorize**</u>: You can play this chord progression pattern in any key as long as you **follow the key signature** of that scale.

Song Example: Ain't Misbehavin'

Example #1

Example #2

Once you have practiced the 7th chords and the Jazz chord progression on the previous page, you can practice using four note **left hand 7th chords** like in Example #1.

Example #2 shows how to add the harmony notes to the **melody in the right hand**. Make sure your harmony notes are notes that are in the chord symbol. If necessary, check the **Chord Speller** in the Reference section for the correct letter names of the chords.

You always have **two choices** for your arrangements:
1) Left hand chords with right hand melody as in Example #1
2) Right hand chords with left hand bass notes as in Example #2

Practice both examples and then try the lead sheets for "Ain't Misbehavin'" and "Give My Regards to Broadway" on the next page, with **both** arrangements.

Ain't Misbehavin'

Razaf/Waller/Brooks

Give My Regards to Broadway

Brightly

George M. Cohan

#20 Song Example:
Are You Lonesome Tonight?

Here are **three different ways** to play this song, made famous by Elvis Presley.

Example #1 is a technique from page 85, expanded left hand patterns with right hand chords.

Example #2 changes the left hand to an "oom pah" pattern from page 46.

Example #3 uses the **jazz style ii7-V7-I7 chord progression** on page 106. If you see the Dm/G7 combination in a fake book song, simply add a "7" to all of the chords. "C" becomes "Cmaj7", "E" becomes "Em7", etc. See page 112 for the C6 chord ending!

Example #1

Example #2

Example #3

Are You Lonesome Tonight?

Moderately

R. Turk and L. Handman

#21 Ending a Song

One of the most important parts of a song is the ending. The ending will add a special touch to your arrangements of songs and pieces of music.

Practice the next three examples and add your chosen ending to your arrangements.

Example #1: C6 Chord

The **C6 chord** is an excellent chord to use at the end of a **swing or jazz-style** song. It adds a jazz flavor to the sound of your arrangement.

A C6 chord is simply a C chord (CEG) with an **A added to the chord**. The A is six notes above C, so it's called a "C6" chord.

If the song is upbeat, you can swing the 8ths, or play straight 8ths if the song is more mellow.

In the example above, the last chord is a C6 chord held for two beats, with a C6 arpeggio going up the piano.

<u>Memorize</u>: When the last melody note is the tonic note (C in the Key of C), play the **C first inversion chord with an A added in the middle**.

Example #2: Csus Chord

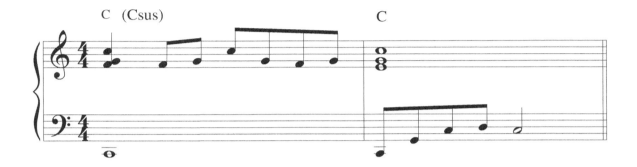

In the Csus chord, the **4th note of the C scale (F)**, is played in place of the 3rd note of the C chord (E). When you play the C chord directly after the Csus chord, the F sounds like it **"resolves down" to E**.

Turn the last measure's C chord, with the C on the top, into a Csus chord to extend the ending one more measure, then resolve the Csus chord to a C major chord (F becomes E).

Example #3: Extended Ending

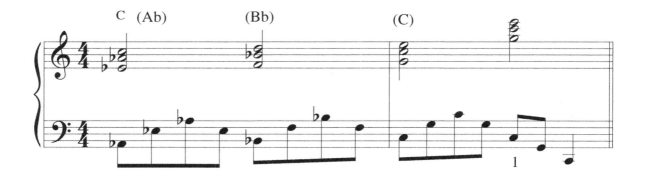

This is an ending that you could use in your song arrangement to make the **end sound "big" or "grand"**.

This ending extends the song by **replacing** the final C chord (C on the top) with an Ab inversion chord. From the Ab chord, step up to Bb chord and finally to the C second inversion chord.

This ending sounds "deceptive" because the chord on the last word of the song is not the tonic chord but a totally **unexpected chord** which will surprise the listener.

Memorize: The C chord and the Ab replacement chord **share the same letter** on the top (C). Only change the bottom two letters to make it an Ab chord.

Reference Section

#1 Note and Rest Values

The chart below shows the most common notes and their relationship to each other. The <u>time value</u> of each note is determined by the **time signature** (see Reference Section #2).

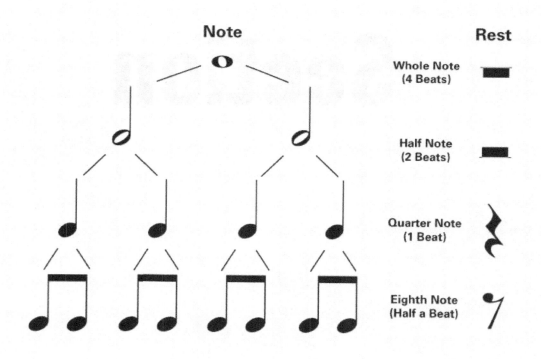

#2 Time Signatures and Playing Hands Together

The two numbers at the beginning of every song/piece are called the **Time Signature**. The time signatures used in most fake books are 3/4, 4/4, 6/8 and 2/2 (cut time).

The top number tells you how many **beats in each measure** and the bottom number tells you which note **gets one beat**.

Two 8th notes equal one quarter note. Practice playing the right hand quarter notes against the left hand 8th note octave pattern.

Repeat this 3 beat pattern of quarter notes against 8th notes.

In cut time, the notes in the measure look like 4/4 time, but are played with a 2 beat feel. Count 1 & 2 & instead.

In 6/8 time, each 8th note is one beat. This time signature has a two beat feel (three 8ths per beat). Repeat this measure and feel the two beats.

#3 The G Clef and F Clef
Lines and Spaces

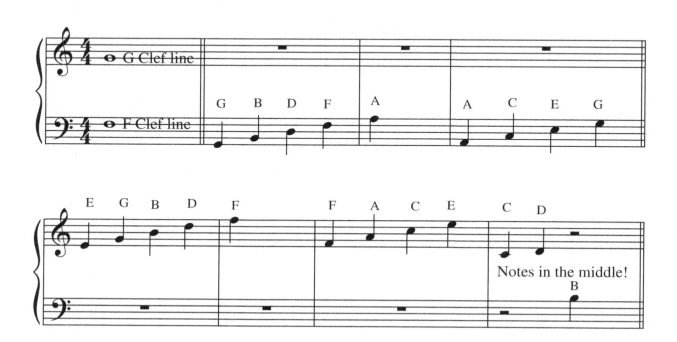

Music is written on a staff of five lines and four spaces.
The bottom line or space is always "line 1" or "space 1".

The **clefs** are at the beginning of each line to indicate
which line is G (G Clef) and which line is F (F Clef). Once
you find the G and F lines, count up or down within the
musical alphabet to figure out the other lines and spaces.

Memorize: Middle C is always in the middle between the
two staves. The G Clef line is **five steps above** middle C
and the F Clef line is **five steps below** middle C.

#4 Half Steps and Whole Steps

The space between two notes is called an <u>interval</u>. A **half step** is the smallest interval and is from one key on the piano to the next closest key, higher or lower, black or white. A **whole step** is made up of two half steps.

Remember that a sharp (#) is the very next key to the **right** (white or black key), and a flat (b) is the very next key to the **left.**

<u>Memorize</u>: A whole step is two keys next to each other that **always** have a key (white or black) in between.

#5 Dictionary of Terms

Listed here are the most common musical terms used in a fake book.

Coda: Ending section

Cut Time: Short for 2/2 time. The half note receives one beat.

D.C. al coda: Return to the beginning, play to the Coda sign, then jump to the Coda.

D.S. al coda: Go back to the dal segno sign, play to the Coda sign, then jump to the Coda.

Interval: the space between two notes, for instance, C to G is the interval of a 5th.

N.C.: No chord

Natural: a symbol that cancels a flat or a sharp note.

Tie: two notes that are the same letter name are tied together with a slur line. The second note is NOT played, hold the first note for the extra value.

Triplet: three eighth notes equal ONE quarter note

1st and 2nd Endings: play the first ending and repeat. Then play the second ending skipping over the first ending.

#6 Chord Speller

C chords

C	C-E-G
Cm	C-Eb-G
C7	C-E-G-Bb
Cdim	C-Eb-Gb
C+	C-E-G#

C# or Db chords

C#	C#-E#-G#
C#m	C#-E-G#
C#7	C#-E#-G#-B
C#dim	C#-E-G
C#+	C#-E#-Gx

D chords

D	D-F#-A
Dm	D-F-A
D7	D-F#-A-C
Ddim	D-F-Ab
D+	D-F#-A#

Eb chords

Eb	Eb-G-Bb
Ebm	Eb-Gb-Bb
E7	Eb-G-Bb-Db
Ebdim	Eb-Gb-Bbb
Eb+	Eb-G-B

E chords

E	E-G#-B
Em	E-G-B
Em7	E-G-B-D
Edim	E-G-Bb
E+	E-G#-B#

F chords

F	F-A-C
Fm	F-Ab-C
F7	F-A-C-Eb
Fdim	F-Ab-Cb
F+	F-A-C#

F# or Gb chords

F#	F#-A#-C#
F#m	F#-A-C#
F#7	F#-A#-C#-E
F#dim	F#-A-C
F#+	F#-A#-Cx

G chords

G	G-B-D
Gm	G-Bb-D
G7	G-B-D-F
Gdim	G-Bb-Db
G+	G-B-D#

Ab chords

Ab	Ab-C-Eb
Abm	Ab-Cb-Eb
Ab7	Ab-C-Eb-Gb
Abdim	Ab-Cb-Ebb
Ab+	Ab-C-E

A chords

A	A-C#-E
Am	A-C-E
A7	A-C#-E-G
Adim	A-C-Eb
A+	A-C#-E#

Bb chords

Bb	Bb-D-F
Bbm	Bb-Db-F
Bb7	Bb-D-F-Ab
Bbdim	Bb-Db-Fb
Bb+	Bb-D-F#

B chords

B	B-D#-F#
Bm	B-D-F#
B7	B-D#-F#-A
Bdim	B-D-F
B+	B-D#-Fx

Note: an "x" denotes double sharp

90900350R00070